45 Milk Recipes for Home

By: Kelly Johnson

Table of Contents

Breakfast:

- Classic French Toast with Vanilla Milk
- Blueberry Pancakes with Buttermilk
- Coconut Milk Chia Pudding
- Cinnamon Roll Overnight Oats with Almond Milk
- Ricotta Stuffed Crepes with Berry Compote
- Vanilla and Honey Yogurt Parfait

Beverages:

- Golden Turmeric Latte with Coconut Milk
- Iced Matcha Latte with Sweetened Condensed Milk
- Horchata – Cinnamon Rice Milk
- Espresso Chocolate Milkshake
- Strawberry-Banana Smoothie with Greek Yogurt
- Lavender-infused Warm Milk

Soups:

- Creamy Tomato Basil Soup with Whole Milk
- Broccoli and Cheddar Soup with Heavy Cream
- Spiced Pumpkin Soup with Coconut Milk
- Creamy Chicken and Wild Rice Soup

Appetizers:

- Spinach and Feta Stuffed Mushrooms with Milk
- Creamy Avocado Lime Dip with Greek Yogurt
- Baked Artichoke Dip with Parmesan and Mayonnaise

Main Courses:

- Creamy Chicken Alfredo Pasta
- Coconut Milk Curry Chicken
- Tuna Casserole with Evaporated Milk

- Creamy Mushroom Risotto with Arborio Rice
- Beef Stroganoff with Sour Cream

Sides:

- Scalloped Potatoes with Gruyère Cheese and Milk
- Creamed Corn with Whole Milk
- Mashed Sweet Potatoes with Brown Sugar and Milk
- Cauliflower Gratin with Parmesan and Milk

Desserts:

- Vanilla Panna Cotta with Berry Compote
- Tres Leches Cake
- Chocolate Pots de Crème
- Rice Pudding with Cinnamon and Raisins
- Coconut Rice Pudding with Mango

Baked Goods:

- Fluffy Buttermilk Biscuits
- Cream Cheese-Filled Banana Bread
- Lemon Poppy Seed Muffins with Greek Yogurt
- Chocolate Zucchini Cake with Sour Cream
- Custard-filled Pastries with Vanilla Glaze

Ice Cream and Frozen Treats:

- Homemade Vanilla Bean Ice Cream
- Strawberry Swirl Frozen Yogurt
- Mint Chocolate Chip Milkshakes

Cocktails:

- White Russian Cocktail with Cream
- Irish Cream Liqueur
- Brandy Alexander with Nutmeg
- Eggnog Martini with Spiced Rum

Breakfast:

Classic French Toast with Vanilla Milk

Ingredients:

- 4 slices of thick-cut bread (brioche or challah works well)
- 2 large eggs
- 1 cup vanilla-flavored milk
- 1 teaspoon pure vanilla extract
- 1/2 teaspoon ground cinnamon
- Pinch of salt
- Butter or cooking spray for greasing the pan
- Maple syrup, powdered sugar, and fresh berries for serving

Instructions:

Prepare the Egg Mixture:
- In a shallow dish, whisk together the eggs, vanilla-flavored milk, vanilla extract, ground cinnamon, and a pinch of salt. Ensure that the mixture is well combined.

Soak the Bread:
- Place each slice of bread into the egg mixture, ensuring that both sides are coated evenly. Allow the bread to soak for about 20-30 seconds on each side.

Heat the Pan:
- Heat a large non-stick skillet or griddle over medium heat. Add a small amount of butter or cooking spray to coat the surface.

Cook the French Toast:
- Carefully transfer the soaked bread slices to the hot skillet. Cook each side until golden brown, usually 2-3 minutes per side.

Serve:
- Once both sides are cooked to perfection, transfer the French toast to a serving plate. Serve immediately with a drizzle of maple syrup, a dusting of powdered sugar, and a handful of fresh berries.

Optional Garnishes:
- Get creative with toppings! Consider adding whipped cream, sliced bananas, chopped nuts, or a sprinkle of cinnamon for extra flavor.

Enjoy:

- Dive into the delightful combination of soft, custardy French toast with the subtle sweetness of vanilla milk. This classic breakfast dish is perfect for a cozy morning or a special brunch.

Note:

- You can use any type of milk, but vanilla-flavored milk adds an extra layer of sweetness and fragrance to the French toast.
- Adjust the level of sweetness by choosing your favorite type of bread and adjusting the amount of vanilla extract accordingly.

Blueberry Pancakes with Buttermilk

Ingredients:

- 1 cup all-purpose flour
- 2 tablespoons sugar
- 1 teaspoon baking powder
- 1/2 teaspoon baking soda
- 1/4 teaspoon salt
- 1 cup buttermilk
- 1 large egg
- 2 tablespoons unsalted butter, melted
- 1 teaspoon vanilla extract
- 1 cup fresh or frozen blueberries
- Butter or cooking spray for the griddle
- Maple syrup for serving

Instructions:

Prepare the Dry Ingredients:
- In a large mixing bowl, whisk together the flour, sugar, baking powder, baking soda, and salt. Ensure that the dry ingredients are well combined.

Mix the Wet Ingredients:
- In a separate bowl, whisk together the buttermilk, egg, melted butter, and vanilla extract until smooth.

Combine Wet and Dry Ingredients:
- Pour the wet ingredients into the bowl with the dry ingredients. Stir until just combined. It's okay if the batter is a bit lumpy; overmixing can make the pancakes tough.

Fold in Blueberries:
- Gently fold in the blueberries, distributing them evenly throughout the batter.

Heat the Griddle:
- Preheat a griddle or non-stick skillet over medium heat. Add a small amount of butter or use cooking spray to coat the surface.

Cook the Pancakes:
- Pour 1/4 cup of batter for each pancake onto the hot griddle. Cook until bubbles form on the surface, and the edges start to look set. Flip the pancakes and cook the other side until golden brown.

Keep Warm:
- As you cook the pancakes, transfer them to a warm oven (around 200°F or 93°C) to keep them warm while you finish the batch.

Serve:
- Serve the blueberry pancakes warm, stacked on a plate. Drizzle with maple syrup and add additional blueberries or a dollop of whipped cream if desired.

Enjoy:
- Delight in the fluffy texture and burst of blueberry sweetness in each bite. These pancakes are a perfect breakfast treat for any day of the week.

Note:

- If using frozen blueberries, toss them in a little flour before adding to the batter to prevent them from sinking to the bottom of the pancakes.
- Adjust the sweetness by adding more or less sugar according to your taste preferences.

Coconut Milk Chia Pudding

Ingredients:

- 1/4 cup chia seeds
- 1 cup coconut milk (full-fat for creaminess)
- 1-2 tablespoons maple syrup or honey (adjust to taste)
- 1/2 teaspoon vanilla extract
- Optional toppings: Fresh berries, sliced fruits, shredded coconut, or nuts

Instructions:

Combine Chia Seeds and Coconut Milk:
- In a bowl or jar, combine chia seeds and coconut milk. Stir well to ensure the chia seeds are evenly distributed.

Add Sweetener and Vanilla:
- Add maple syrup (or honey) and vanilla extract to the mixture. Stir again to combine. Taste and adjust the sweetness if needed.

Mix Well and Refrigerate:
- Mix everything thoroughly to prevent clumps of chia seeds. Cover the bowl or jar and refrigerate for at least 4 hours or overnight. Stir again after the first 30 minutes to avoid clumping.

Check Consistency:
- After the pudding has chilled, check the consistency. If it's too thick, you can add a bit more coconut milk and stir until well combined.

Serve:
- Spoon the coconut milk chia pudding into serving bowls or glasses.

Add Toppings:
- Customize your pudding by adding your favorite toppings. Fresh berries, sliced fruits, shredded coconut, or nuts work well.

Enjoy:
- Dive into the creamy and nutritious goodness of coconut milk chia pudding. It's a delightful treat for breakfast, snack, or dessert.

Note:

- Adjust the sweetness to your liking by varying the amount of maple syrup or honey.

- Experiment with different toppings like mango, pineapple, or passion fruit to enhance the tropical flavors of the coconut milk pudding.
- This recipe can be easily doubled or tripled to make a larger batch for meal prep.

Cinnamon Roll Overnight Oats with Almond Milk

Ingredients:

- 1/2 cup rolled oats
- 1/2 cup unsweetened almond milk
- 1/2 teaspoon ground cinnamon
- 1 tablespoon maple syrup or honey
- 1/4 teaspoon vanilla extract
- 1 tablespoon raisins or chopped nuts (optional)
- Cream cheese glaze:
    - 2 tablespoons cream cheese, softened
    - 1 tablespoon powdered sugar
    - 1-2 tablespoons almond milk (adjust for desired consistency)

Instructions:

For the Overnight Oats:

Combine Ingredients:
- In a jar or airtight container, combine rolled oats, almond milk, ground cinnamon, maple syrup (or honey), and vanilla extract.

Mix Well:
- Stir the ingredients until well combined. Ensure that the oats are fully submerged in the almond milk.

Add Optional Ingredients:
- If desired, mix in raisins or chopped nuts for added texture and flavor.

Refrigerate Overnight:
- Cover the jar or container and refrigerate the mixture overnight or for at least 4-6 hours to allow the oats to soak and soften.

For the Cream Cheese Glaze:

Prepare the Glaze:
- In a small bowl, whisk together softened cream cheese, powdered sugar, and almond milk until smooth. Adjust the almond milk quantity for your preferred drizzling consistency.

Assembling:

Drizzle the Glaze:
- Once the oats have soaked and are ready to be served, drizzle the cream cheese glaze over the top.

Stir and Enjoy:
- Give the oats a good stir, ensuring that the glaze is evenly distributed. The oats can be enjoyed cold or warmed up in the microwave for a cozy breakfast.

Optional Garnish:
- Garnish with an extra sprinkle of cinnamon, a drizzle of maple syrup, or additional nuts if desired.

Savor the Flavors:
- Delight in the delicious taste of cinnamon roll-inspired overnight oats with the creaminess of almond milk. It's a convenient and tasty breakfast option, perfect for those busy mornings.

Note:

- Adjust the sweetness of the oats and glaze according to your preference.
- Feel free to get creative with additional toppings such as sliced bananas, diced apples, or a sprinkle of chopped pecans.

Ricotta Stuffed Crepes with Berry Compote

Ingredients:

For the Crepes:

- 1 cup all-purpose flour
- 2 large eggs
- 1 1/4 cups whole milk
- 2 tablespoons melted unsalted butter
- 1 tablespoon sugar
- 1/4 teaspoon salt

For the Ricotta Filling:

- 1 cup ricotta cheese
- 2 tablespoons powdered sugar
- 1 teaspoon vanilla extract
- Zest of one lemon (optional)

For the Berry Compote:

- 1 cup mixed berries (strawberries, blueberries, raspberries)
- 2 tablespoons sugar
- 1 tablespoon lemon juice
- 1/2 teaspoon vanilla extract

Instructions:

For the Crepes:

Prepare the Batter:
- In a blender, combine the flour, eggs, whole milk, melted butter, sugar, and salt. Blend until the batter is smooth. Let it rest for at least 30 minutes.

Cook the Crepes:
- Heat a non-stick skillet over medium heat. Pour a small amount of batter into the pan, swirling it to coat the bottom evenly. Cook for about 1-2 minutes per side, or until lightly golden. Repeat until all the batter is used, stacking the crepes on a plate.

For the Ricotta Filling:

Prepare the Ricotta Mixture:
- In a bowl, mix together the ricotta cheese, powdered sugar, vanilla extract, and lemon zest (if using). Set aside.

For the Berry Compote:

Cook the Berries:
- In a saucepan, combine the mixed berries, sugar, lemon juice, and vanilla extract. Cook over medium heat, stirring occasionally, until the berries break down and the mixture thickens slightly (about 5-7 minutes).

Assemble the Crepes:
- Spoon a generous dollop of the ricotta mixture onto each crepe and spread it evenly. Fold or roll the crepes as desired.

Serve with Berry Compote:
- Place the stuffed crepes on serving plates and top with the warm berry compote.

Optional Garnish:
- Garnish with a dusting of powdered sugar, extra berries, or a drizzle of honey for added sweetness.

Enjoy:
- Indulge in the delightful combination of tender crepes filled with creamy ricotta and topped with a vibrant berry compote. It's a perfect brunch or dessert option for a touch of elegance and flavor.

Vanilla and Honey Yogurt Parfait

Ingredients:

- 2 cups Greek yogurt (or your favorite yogurt)
- 2 teaspoons pure vanilla extract
- 2 tablespoons honey (plus extra for drizzling)
- 1 cup granola
- 1 cup mixed berries (strawberries, blueberries, raspberries)
- Fresh mint leaves for garnish (optional)

Instructions:

Vanilla Yogurt:
- In a bowl, combine the Greek yogurt, pure vanilla extract, and honey. Mix well until the vanilla and honey are evenly incorporated into the yogurt.

Assemble the Parfaits:
- Begin layering the parfait by spooning a dollop of the vanilla yogurt into the bottom of each serving glass or bowl.

Add Granola Layer:
- Sprinkle a layer of granola over the vanilla yogurt. This adds a delightful crunch and texture to the parfait.

Layer with Berries:
- Add a layer of mixed berries on top of the granola. Use a combination of strawberries, blueberries, and raspberries for a burst of color and flavor.

Repeat Layers:
- Repeat the layering process until you reach the top of the glass or bowl, finishing with a final layer of berries.

Drizzle with Honey:
- Drizzle a little honey over the top of each parfait for added sweetness. Adjust the amount according to your taste preferences.

Garnish (Optional):
- Garnish the parfaits with fresh mint leaves for a touch of freshness and visual appeal.

Chill or Serve Immediately:
- Refrigerate the parfaits for at least 30 minutes to allow the flavors to meld, or serve immediately for a refreshing treat.

Serve and Enjoy:

- Present these visually appealing and delicious Vanilla and Honey Yogurt Parfaits at breakfast, brunch, or as a light and satisfying dessert.

Note:

- Customize the parfait by adding layers of sliced bananas, diced mango, or any other favorite fruits.
- Feel free to experiment with different types of granola or nuts for added variety in texture and flavor.
- This parfait can be a versatile and healthy option, suitable for various dietary preferences.

Beverages:

Golden Turmeric Latte with Coconut Milk

Ingredients:

- 1 cup coconut milk (unsweetened)
- 1 teaspoon ground turmeric
- 1/2 teaspoon ground cinnamon
- 1/4 teaspoon ground ginger
- 1/4 teaspoon vanilla extract
- 1-2 tablespoons honey or maple syrup (adjust to taste)
- Pinch of black pepper (enhances turmeric absorption)
- Optional: Dash of ground cardamom or nutmeg for extra flavor
- Optional: Coconut whipped cream for garnish

Instructions:

Warm Coconut Milk:
- In a small saucepan, gently heat the coconut milk over medium heat. Avoid boiling; aim for a warm but not scalding temperature.

Mix in Turmeric and Spices:
- Whisk in the ground turmeric, ground cinnamon, ground ginger, and black pepper. Continue to whisk until the spices are well combined.

Add Vanilla Extract:
- Stir in the vanilla extract, ensuring it is evenly distributed throughout the mixture.

Sweeten the Latte:
- Add honey or maple syrup to sweeten the latte. Adjust the sweetness according to your taste preferences.

Blend Well:
- Whisk or blend the mixture thoroughly to create a smooth and well-mixed golden turmeric latte.

Strain (Optional):
- If you prefer a smoother texture, strain the latte through a fine mesh sieve or cheesecloth to remove any residue.

Pour and Garnish:
- Pour the golden turmeric latte into your favorite mug. Optionally, top it with coconut whipped cream and a sprinkle of ground cardamom or nutmeg.

Enjoy:
- Sip and savor the comforting warmth and unique flavors of this golden turmeric latte with coconut milk. It's not only delicious but also rich in anti-inflammatory properties.

Note:

- Turmeric can stain, so be cautious when handling it, and clean any utensils promptly.
- Adjust the spice quantities to suit your taste preferences. Some may prefer a stronger ginger or cinnamon flavor.
- Experiment with different plant-based sweeteners, like agave syrup or date syrup, for alternative sweetness.

Iced Matcha Latte with Sweetened Condensed Milk

Ingredients:

- 1 teaspoon matcha powder
- 2 tablespoons hot water
- 1 cup milk of your choice (dairy or plant-based)
- Ice cubes
- 2 tablespoons sweetened condensed milk
- Optional: Vanilla extract or vanilla syrup for added flavor
- Optional: Whipped cream for topping

Instructions:

Prepare Matcha Paste:
- In a bowl, whisk the matcha powder with hot water until it forms a smooth paste. Ensure there are no lumps.

Heat and Froth Milk:
- Heat the milk on the stove or in the microwave until it's warm but not boiling. Froth the milk using a milk frother or by vigorously shaking it in a sealed container.

Combine Matcha and Milk:
- Pour the matcha paste into a glass. Add the warm frothed milk over the matcha paste and stir well to combine.

Sweeten with Condensed Milk:
- Add sweetened condensed milk to the matcha-milk mixture. Adjust the quantity based on your desired level of sweetness. Stir until the condensed milk is fully incorporated.

Add Ice Cubes:
- Fill the glass with ice cubes to chill the iced matcha latte.

Optional Vanilla Flavor:
- If desired, add a splash of vanilla extract or vanilla syrup to enhance the flavor. Stir well.

Top with Whipped Cream (Optional):
- For an indulgent touch, top the iced matcha latte with a dollop of whipped cream.

Stir and Enjoy:

- Stir the iced matcha latte well to ensure all the flavors are mixed. Sip and enjoy the refreshing combination of matcha and sweetened condensed milk.

Note:

- Adjust the sweetness by varying the amount of sweetened condensed milk according to your taste preferences.
- You can use any type of milk, including dairy or plant-based alternatives like almond milk, soy milk, or coconut milk.
- Experiment with different flavored syrups or extracts to customize the latte to your liking.

Horchata – Cinnamon Rice Milk

Ingredients:

- 1 cup long-grain white rice
- 3 cinnamon sticks
- 4 cups water
- 1 cup milk of your choice (dairy or plant-based)
- 3/4 cup granulated sugar (adjust to taste)
- 1 teaspoon vanilla extract
- Ground cinnamon for garnish
- Ice cubes for serving

Instructions:

Rinse and Soak Rice:
- Rinse the white rice under cold water until the water runs clear. Place the rinsed rice in a bowl with 2 cinnamon sticks and cover it with 2 cups of water. Allow it to soak for at least 6 hours or overnight.

Blend Rice and Cinnamon:
- After soaking, discard the cinnamon sticks. Transfer the rice and remaining water to a blender. Blend until you get a smooth, liquid consistency.

Strain the Mixture:
- Strain the blended rice mixture through a fine-mesh sieve, cheesecloth, or a nut milk bag into a large bowl or pitcher. Use the back of a spoon to press out as much liquid as possible.

Add Milk and Sweeten:
- Stir in the milk of your choice (dairy or plant-based) into the strained rice mixture. Add granulated sugar and vanilla extract. Mix well until the sugar is dissolved. Adjust sweetness to your liking.

Chill the Horchata:
- Refrigerate the horchata for at least 2 hours to allow the flavors to meld and the mixture to chill.

Serve Over Ice:
- When ready to serve, fill glasses with ice cubes and pour the chilled horchata over the ice.

Garnish and Enjoy:

- Garnish the horchata with a sprinkle of ground cinnamon on top. Stir before drinking to make sure the flavors are well-distributed.

Optional: Cinnamon Stick Garnish:
- Add a cinnamon stick to each glass for an extra touch of presentation and flavor.

Sip and Relax:
- Enjoy the refreshing and subtly sweet taste of homemade horchata, a delightful beverage with a hint of cinnamon and vanilla.

Note:

- Adjust the sugar content to your taste preference. You can start with less sugar and add more if needed.
- Shake or stir the horchata before serving if it separates while chilling in the refrigerator.
- Horchata is best served cold over ice.

Espresso Chocolate Milkshake

Ingredients:

- 1 cup vanilla ice cream
- 1/2 cup cold brewed espresso or strongly brewed coffee, chilled
- 1/2 cup milk (dairy or plant-based)
- 2 tablespoons chocolate syrup
- 1 tablespoon unsweetened cocoa powder
- 1-2 tablespoons granulated sugar (optional, depending on sweetness preference)
- Whipped cream for topping
- Chocolate shavings or cocoa powder for garnish

Instructions:

Brew Espresso or Coffee:
- Brew a strong cup of espresso or coffee and let it chill in the refrigerator until cold.

Prepare the Blender:
- In a blender, add vanilla ice cream, cold brewed espresso or coffee, milk, chocolate syrup, unsweetened cocoa powder, and granulated sugar (if using).

Blend Until Smooth:
- Blend the ingredients on high speed until you achieve a smooth and creamy consistency.

Taste and Adjust:
- Taste the milkshake and adjust the sweetness or thickness by adding more sugar or milk, if necessary. Blend again to incorporate any adjustments.

Prepare Serving Glasses:
- Drizzle the inside of serving glasses with a little chocolate syrup for a decorative touch.

Pour and Top:
- Pour the espresso chocolate milkshake into the prepared glasses. Top each milkshake with a generous dollop of whipped cream.

Garnish:
- Garnish the whipped cream with chocolate shavings or a sprinkle of cocoa powder for an extra chocolatey touch.

Serve Immediately:

- Serve the espresso chocolate milkshake immediately while it's cold and the whipped cream is still fluffy.

Enjoy:
- Sip and savor the rich and indulgent flavors of this Espresso Chocolate Milkshake. It's a delightful treat for coffee and chocolate lovers alike.

Note:

- You can customize the sweetness by adjusting the amount of sugar and chocolate syrup based on your taste preferences.
- For an adult version, you can add a splash of coffee liqueur or chocolate liqueur to the milkshake.

Strawberry-Banana Smoothie with Greek Yogurt

Ingredients:

- 1 cup frozen strawberries
- 1 ripe banana, peeled and sliced
- 1/2 cup Greek yogurt
- 1/2 cup milk (dairy or plant-based)
- 1 tablespoon honey or maple syrup (optional, depending on sweetness preference)
- 1/2 teaspoon vanilla extract
- Ice cubes (optional)
- Fresh strawberries and banana slices for garnish

Instructions:

Prepare the Ingredients:
- Wash and hull the strawberries. Peel and slice the ripe banana.

Assemble in Blender:
- In a blender, combine the frozen strawberries, banana slices, Greek yogurt, milk, honey (if using), and vanilla extract.

Blend Until Smooth:
- Blend the ingredients on high speed until the mixture becomes smooth and creamy. If you prefer a thicker consistency, you can add ice cubes and blend again.

Taste and Adjust:
- Taste the smoothie and adjust the sweetness by adding more honey or sweetener of choice, if needed. Blend again to incorporate any adjustments.

Prepare Serving Glasses:
- If desired, run a slice of fresh strawberry along the rim of each serving glass for a decorative touch.

Pour and Garnish:
- Pour the strawberry-banana smoothie into the prepared glasses. Garnish with fresh strawberry slices and banana slices.

Serve Immediately:
- Serve the smoothie immediately while it's cold and refreshing.

Enjoy:

- Indulge in the delicious and nutritious Strawberry-Banana Smoothie with Greek Yogurt. It's a delightful and satisfying beverage perfect for breakfast or a snack.

Note:

- Feel free to customize the smoothie by adding a handful of spinach or kale for a green boost without altering the flavor significantly.
- You can use any type of milk or yogurt based on your dietary preferences.
- Adjust the sweetness to your liking by experimenting with different sweeteners or adjusting the quantity of honey or maple syrup.

Lavender-infused Warm Milk

Ingredients:

- 1 cup milk (dairy or plant-based)
- 1 teaspoon dried culinary lavender buds
- 1-2 tablespoons honey or sweetener of choice (optional)
- 1/4 teaspoon vanilla extract (optional)
- Pinch of ground cinnamon (optional)

Instructions:

Heat the Milk:
- In a small saucepan, heat the milk over medium heat until it begins to steam. Do not let it boil; aim for a warm temperature.

Infuse with Lavender:
- Add the dried culinary lavender buds to the warm milk. Stir gently to immerse the lavender in the milk.

Steep the Lavender:
- Let the lavender steep in the warm milk for about 5-7 minutes. This allows the aromatic flavors of the lavender to infuse into the milk.

Strain the Lavender:
- After steeping, strain the lavender-infused milk through a fine-mesh sieve or cheesecloth into a cup or mug. This removes the lavender buds, leaving behind the infused milk.

Sweeten and Flavor (Optional):
- Add honey or sweetener of choice to the lavender-infused milk, adjusting the sweetness according to your preference. Optionally, add vanilla extract for extra flavor and a pinch of ground cinnamon for warmth.

Stir Well:
- Stir the lavender-infused warm milk thoroughly to incorporate the sweetener and optional flavorings.

Serve:
- Pour the lavender-infused warm milk into a cup or mug.

Optional Garnish:
- Garnish with a sprinkle of dried lavender buds on top for a decorative touch.

Sip and Relax:

- Enjoy the soothing and aromatic experience of lavender-infused warm milk. This calming beverage is perfect for winding down before bedtime or for a moment of relaxation during the day.

Note:

- Adjust the sweetness and flavorings to suit your taste preferences.
- Use culinary-grade lavender to ensure it is safe for consumption. You can find dried culinary lavender in specialty stores or online.

Soups:

Creamy Tomato Basil Soup with Whole Milk

Ingredients:

- 2 tablespoons olive oil
- 1 medium onion, finely chopped
- 2 cloves garlic, minced
- 1 can (28 ounces) whole peeled tomatoes
- 1 cup tomato sauce
- 1 cup vegetable or chicken broth
- 1 teaspoon dried basil
- 1/2 teaspoon dried oregano
- Salt and pepper to taste
- 1 cup whole milk
- 2 tablespoons tomato paste
- 2 tablespoons unsalted butter (optional, for extra richness)
- Fresh basil leaves for garnish
- Grated Parmesan cheese for garnish (optional)
- Croutons or crusty bread for serving

Instructions:

Sauté Onions and Garlic:
- In a large pot, heat olive oil over medium heat. Add finely chopped onions and minced garlic. Sauté until the onions are soft and translucent.

Add Tomatoes and Sauce:
- Pour in the whole peeled tomatoes, tomato sauce, and tomato paste. Break up the whole tomatoes with a spoon. Stir to combine.

Season with Herbs and Broth:
- Add dried basil, dried oregano, salt, and pepper to the pot. Pour in the vegetable or chicken broth. Stir well and bring the mixture to a simmer.

Simmer and Blend:
- Let the soup simmer for about 15-20 minutes to allow the flavors to meld. Use an immersion blender to blend the soup until smooth. Alternatively, transfer the soup in batches to a blender and blend until smooth, then return it to the pot.

Add Whole Milk:
- Pour in the whole milk and stir to combine. Add unsalted butter if desired for an extra creamy texture.

Adjust Seasoning:
- Taste the soup and adjust the seasoning if needed. Add more salt, pepper, or herbs according to your preference.

Simmer and Serve:
- Allow the soup to simmer for an additional 10-15 minutes over low heat, stirring occasionally. This helps the flavors further develop.

Garnish and Serve:
- Ladle the creamy tomato basil soup into bowls. Garnish with fresh basil leaves and, if desired, grated Parmesan cheese. Serve with croutons or crusty bread.

Enjoy:
- Enjoy the comforting and rich flavor of the Creamy Tomato Basil Soup with Whole Milk. It's a perfect meal on its own or paired with your favorite bread.

Note:

- Adjust the consistency by adding more broth if you prefer a thinner soup.
- Customize the soup by adding a touch of heavy cream or grated Parmesan for additional richness.
- Fresh basil adds a burst of flavor; add it just before serving for the best taste.

Broccoli and Cheddar Soup with Heavy Cream

Ingredients:

- 2 tablespoons unsalted butter
- 1 onion, chopped
- 2 cloves garlic, minced
- 3 cups broccoli florets, chopped
- 3 cups vegetable or chicken broth
- 1 cup heavy cream
- 2 cups shredded sharp cheddar cheese
- 1/4 cup all-purpose flour
- Salt and pepper to taste
- Pinch of nutmeg (optional, for added depth)
- Croutons or crusty bread for serving (optional)

Instructions:

Sauté Onions and Garlic:
- In a large pot, melt the butter over medium heat. Add the chopped onion and minced garlic. Sauté until the onions are soft and translucent.

Add Broccoli:
- Add the chopped broccoli florets to the pot. Stir and cook for a few minutes until the broccoli starts to soften.

Make Roux:
- Sprinkle the flour over the vegetables, stirring continuously to create a roux. Cook for 2-3 minutes to eliminate the raw flour taste.

Add Broth:
- Gradually pour in the vegetable or chicken broth while stirring to avoid lumps. Bring the mixture to a simmer and let it cook until the broccoli is tender.

Blend Soup:
- Use an immersion blender to blend the soup until smooth. Alternatively, transfer the soup in batches to a blender and blend until smooth, then return it to the pot.

Add Heavy Cream:
- Pour in the heavy cream and stir well to combine. Allow the soup to simmer for a few more minutes.

Add Cheddar Cheese:

- Gradually add the shredded cheddar cheese to the soup, stirring continuously until the cheese is melted and incorporated into the soup.

Season:
- Season the soup with salt, pepper, and a pinch of nutmeg if desired. Adjust the seasoning according to your taste.

Simmer and Serve:
- Let the soup simmer for an additional 5-10 minutes over low heat to allow the flavors to meld.

Garnish and Serve:
- Ladle the Broccoli and Cheddar Soup into bowls. Optionally, garnish with extra shredded cheddar cheese and serve with croutons or crusty bread.

Enjoy:
- Enjoy the rich and comforting Broccoli and Cheddar Soup with Heavy Cream. It's a delicious bowl of warmth, perfect for a cozy meal.

Note:

- For a smoother texture, blend the soup until it reaches your desired consistency.
- Adjust the amount of heavy cream for a creamier or lighter soup.
- Customize by adding a dash of hot sauce or Worcestershire sauce for an extra flavor kick.

Spiced Pumpkin Soup with Coconut Milk

Ingredients:

- 2 tablespoons olive oil
- 1 onion, chopped
- 3 cloves garlic, minced
- 1 teaspoon ground cumin
- 1/2 teaspoon ground coriander
- 1/2 teaspoon ground ginger
- 1/4 teaspoon cayenne pepper (adjust to taste)
- 4 cups pumpkin puree (canned or homemade)
- 4 cups vegetable or chicken broth
- 1 can (14 ounces) coconut milk
- Salt and black pepper to taste
- 1 tablespoon maple syrup or honey (optional, for sweetness)
- Fresh cilantro or parsley for garnish (optional)
- Pumpkin seeds for topping (optional)

Instructions:

Sauté Onions and Garlic:
- In a large pot, heat olive oil over medium heat. Add chopped onions and cook until softened. Add minced garlic and sauté for an additional minute.

Add Spices:
- Stir in ground cumin, ground coriander, ground ginger, and cayenne pepper. Cook for another minute to toast the spices and release their flavors.

Incorporate Pumpkin Puree:
- Add the pumpkin puree to the pot, stirring well to combine with the spices and onions.

Pour in Broth:
- Pour in the vegetable or chicken broth, stirring continuously to create a smooth mixture.

Simmer:
- Allow the soup to simmer for about 15-20 minutes to let the flavors meld and the pumpkin cook thoroughly.

Add Coconut Milk:
- Pour in the coconut milk, stirring to combine. Simmer for an additional 5-10 minutes.

Season:
- Season the soup with salt and black pepper to taste. Add maple syrup or honey if you prefer a touch of sweetness. Adjust the seasoning according to your preference.

Blend (Optional):
- For a smoother texture, use an immersion blender to blend the soup directly in the pot. Alternatively, transfer the soup in batches to a blender and blend until smooth, then return it to the pot.

Serve:
- Ladle the Spiced Pumpkin Soup into bowls.

Garnish:
- Garnish with fresh cilantro or parsley and pumpkin seeds if desired.

Enjoy:
- Savor the warming and flavorful Spiced Pumpkin Soup with Coconut Milk. It's a delightful autumn dish that brings comfort and richness to your table.

Note:

- Adjust the level of cayenne pepper based on your spice preference.
- The addition of maple syrup or honey is optional and can be adjusted according to your taste for a hint of sweetness.
- For added creaminess, you can stir in a couple of tablespoons of coconut cream before serving.

Creamy Chicken and Wild Rice Soup

Ingredients:

- 1 cup wild rice blend
- 2 tablespoons olive oil or butter
- 1 onion, finely chopped
- 3 carrots, diced
- 3 celery stalks, diced
- 3 cloves garlic, minced
- 1 teaspoon dried thyme
- 1 teaspoon dried rosemary
- 1/2 teaspoon dried sage
- Salt and black pepper to taste
- 1/4 cup all-purpose flour
- 4 cups chicken broth
- 2 cups cooked chicken, shredded or diced
- 1 cup half-and-half or heavy cream
- Fresh parsley for garnish (optional)

Instructions:

Cook Wild Rice:
- Cook the wild rice blend according to the package instructions. Set aside.

Sauté Vegetables:
- In a large pot, heat olive oil or butter over medium heat. Add chopped onion, diced carrots, and diced celery. Sauté until the vegetables are softened.

Add Garlic and Herbs:
- Add minced garlic, dried thyme, dried rosemary, dried sage, salt, and black pepper. Stir and cook for an additional 1-2 minutes until the garlic is fragrant.

Make Roux:
- Sprinkle the flour over the sautéed vegetables, stirring continuously to create a roux. Cook for 2-3 minutes to eliminate the raw flour taste.

Pour in Chicken Broth:
- Gradually pour in the chicken broth, stirring continuously to avoid lumps. Bring the mixture to a simmer.

Add Cooked Chicken and Rice:

- Add the cooked chicken and the prepared wild rice to the pot. Stir well to combine.

Simmer:
- Let the soup simmer for about 15-20 minutes, allowing the flavors to meld and the soup to thicken slightly.

Add Cream:
- Pour in the half-and-half or heavy cream, stirring to combine. Let the soup simmer for an additional 5-10 minutes.

Adjust Seasoning:
- Taste the soup and adjust the seasoning if needed. Add more salt and pepper according to your taste.

Serve:
- Ladle the Creamy Chicken and Wild Rice Soup into bowls.

Garnish:
- Garnish with fresh parsley if desired.

Enjoy:
- Enjoy the comforting and hearty Creamy Chicken and Wild Rice Soup. It's a perfect meal for cooler days.

Note:

- You can use a pre-cooked rotisserie chicken or leftover roasted chicken for added convenience.
- Customize the soup by adding vegetables like mushrooms or peas for additional flavor and texture.

Appetizers:

Spinach and Feta Stuffed Mushrooms with Milk

Ingredients:

- 20 large mushrooms, cleaned and stems removed
- 1 tablespoon olive oil
- 1 small onion, finely chopped
- 2 cloves garlic, minced
- 2 cups fresh spinach, chopped
- 1/2 cup feta cheese, crumbled
- 1/4 cup grated Parmesan cheese
- 1/4 cup milk
- Salt and pepper to taste
- 1/4 teaspoon red pepper flakes (optional)
- Fresh parsley for garnish

Instructions:

Preheat Oven:
- Preheat the oven to 375°F (190°C).

Prepare Mushrooms:
- Clean the mushrooms and remove the stems. Place the mushroom caps on a baking sheet, ready for stuffing.

Sauté Onion and Garlic:
- In a skillet, heat olive oil over medium heat. Add chopped onion and sauté until softened. Add minced garlic and cook for an additional 1-2 minutes until fragrant.

Add Spinach:
- Add chopped spinach to the skillet and sauté until wilted. Remove the skillet from heat.

Prepare Filling:
- In a bowl, combine the sautéed spinach mixture with crumbled feta cheese, grated Parmesan cheese, milk, salt, pepper, and red pepper flakes (if using). Mix well to create the stuffing.

Stuff Mushrooms:
- Spoon the spinach and feta mixture into the mushroom caps, pressing the filling down gently.

Bake:
- Bake the stuffed mushrooms in the preheated oven for 15-20 minutes or until the mushrooms are tender and the filling is golden brown.

Garnish and Serve:
- Remove the stuffed mushrooms from the oven and garnish with fresh parsley. Serve warm.

Enjoy:
- Delight in these Spinach and Feta Stuffed Mushrooms with Milk as a flavorful appetizer or a tasty snack.

Note:

- You can experiment with different types of mushrooms for this recipe, such as cremini or baby bella mushrooms.
- Adjust the level of red pepper flakes based on your spice preference.
- Feel free to add a touch of nutmeg or your favorite herbs to enhance the flavor of the stuffing.

Creamy Avocado Lime Dip with Greek Yogurt

Ingredients:

- 2 ripe avocados, peeled and pitted
- 1 cup Greek yogurt
- 1-2 cloves garlic, minced
- Juice of 1 lime
- 2 tablespoons fresh cilantro, chopped
- Salt and pepper to taste
- Optional: 1/2 teaspoon cumin for added flavor
- Optional: Red pepper flakes for a hint of heat

Instructions:

Prepare Avocados:
- In a bowl, mash the ripe avocados with a fork until smooth.

Add Greek Yogurt:
- Incorporate the Greek yogurt into the mashed avocados, mixing well to combine.

Minced Garlic:
- Add minced garlic to the mixture. Adjust the quantity based on your preference for garlic flavor.

Squeeze Lime:
- Squeeze the juice of one lime into the bowl, ensuring to catch any seeds. Lime adds a bright and zesty flavor to the dip.

Add Cilantro:
- Stir in chopped cilantro for a burst of fresh herb flavor.

Season:
- Season the creamy avocado lime dip with salt and pepper to taste. If desired, add cumin for an extra layer of flavor.

Optional Heat:
- For those who enjoy a bit of heat, sprinkle in red pepper flakes. Adjust the quantity based on your spice preference.

Mix Thoroughly:
- Mix all the ingredients thoroughly until well combined.

Chill (Optional):
- For enhanced flavor, refrigerate the dip for at least 30 minutes before serving. This allows the ingredients to meld and the flavors to develop.

Serve:
- Serve the Creamy Avocado Lime Dip with Greek Yogurt in a bowl, garnished with additional cilantro if desired.

Enjoy:
- Enjoy this delightful and nutritious dip with tortilla chips, fresh vegetable sticks, or as a topping for tacos and salads.

Note:

- Adjust the quantities of lime, garlic, and cilantro to suit your taste preferences.
- This versatile dip can be customized with additional ingredients like diced tomatoes, red onions, or jalapeños for added texture and flavor.

Baked Artichoke Dip with Parmesan and Mayonnaise

Ingredients:

- 1 can (14 ounces) artichoke hearts, drained and chopped
- 1 cup mayonnaise
- 1 cup grated Parmesan cheese
- 1 cup shredded mozzarella cheese
- 1/2 cup sour cream
- 1/4 cup grated Romano cheese
- 2 cloves garlic, minced
- 1/2 teaspoon dried oregano
- 1/2 teaspoon dried basil
- 1/4 teaspoon garlic powder
- 1/4 teaspoon onion powder
- Salt and black pepper to taste
- Dash of cayenne pepper (optional, for a hint of heat)
- Fresh parsley for garnish
- Tortilla chips, crackers, or sliced baguette for serving

Instructions:

Preheat Oven:
- Preheat the oven to 375°F (190°C).

Prepare Artichokes:
- Drain and chop the artichoke hearts.

Mix Ingredients:
- In a mixing bowl, combine the chopped artichoke hearts, mayonnaise, grated Parmesan cheese, shredded mozzarella cheese, sour cream, grated Romano cheese, minced garlic, dried oregano, dried basil, garlic powder, onion powder, salt, black pepper, and cayenne pepper (if using). Mix well to ensure all ingredients are evenly combined.

Transfer to Baking Dish:
- Transfer the mixture to a baking dish, spreading it evenly.

Bake:
- Bake in the preheated oven for 25-30 minutes or until the dip is hot, bubbly, and golden brown on top.

Garnish:

- Remove the baked artichoke dip from the oven and garnish with fresh parsley.

Serve:
- Allow the dip to cool slightly before serving. Serve with tortilla chips, crackers, or sliced baguette.

Enjoy:
- Enjoy this savory and creamy Baked Artichoke Dip with Parmesan and Mayonnaise as a crowd-pleasing appetizer at your gatherings.

Note:

- Adjust the seasoning and cheese quantities to suit your taste preferences.
- Feel free to add diced green onions or a squeeze of lemon juice for added freshness.
- Customize the level of heat by adjusting the amount of cayenne pepper or adding chopped jalapeños if you like it spicy.

Main Courses:

Creamy Chicken Alfredo Pasta

Ingredients:

- 8 ounces fettuccine pasta
- 2 tablespoons unsalted butter
- 1 pound boneless, skinless chicken breast, cut into bite-sized pieces
- Salt and black pepper to taste
- 3 cloves garlic, minced
- 1 cup heavy cream
- 1 cup grated Parmesan cheese
- 1/2 cup grated mozzarella cheese
- 1/2 teaspoon garlic powder
- 1/2 teaspoon onion powder
- 1/2 teaspoon dried Italian seasoning (optional)
- Fresh parsley, chopped, for garnish

Instructions:

Cook Fettuccine:
- Cook the fettuccine pasta according to the package instructions in a large pot of salted boiling water. Drain and set aside.

Sauté Chicken:
- In a large skillet, melt the butter over medium-high heat. Season the chicken pieces with salt and black pepper. Add the chicken to the skillet and cook until browned and cooked through. Remove the chicken from the skillet and set aside.

Cook Garlic:
- In the same skillet, add minced garlic and sauté for about 1 minute until fragrant.

Prepare Alfredo Sauce:
- Pour in the heavy cream, grated Parmesan cheese, grated mozzarella cheese, garlic powder, onion powder, and dried Italian seasoning (if using). Stir continuously until the cheeses are melted and the sauce is smooth.

Combine Chicken and Pasta:
- Add the cooked chicken back into the skillet with the Alfredo sauce. Stir to combine and let it simmer for a few minutes to heat through.

Add Fettuccine:
- Add the cooked fettuccine to the skillet, tossing to coat the pasta evenly with the creamy Alfredo sauce.

Season and Garnish:
- Season with additional salt and black pepper to taste. Garnish with fresh chopped parsley.

Serve:
- Serve the Creamy Chicken Alfredo Pasta hot, garnished with extra Parmesan cheese if desired.

Enjoy:
- Enjoy this indulgent and satisfying dish as a comforting meal for any occasion.

Note:

- You can add vegetables like broccoli or peas for added color and nutrition.
- Adjust the thickness of the Alfredo sauce by adding more or less heavy cream according to your preference.
- Customize the seasoning with your favorite herbs and spices.

Coconut Milk Curry Chicken

Ingredients:

- 1.5 lbs (about 700g) boneless, skinless chicken thighs or breasts, cut into bite-sized pieces
- 2 tablespoons vegetable oil
- 1 large onion, finely chopped
- 3 cloves garlic, minced
- 1 tablespoon ginger, minced
- 2 tablespoons curry powder
- 1 teaspoon ground turmeric
- 1 teaspoon ground cumin
- 1 teaspoon ground coriander
- 1 can (14 ounces) coconut milk
- 1 cup chicken broth
- 1 large potato, peeled and diced
- 1 large carrot, peeled and sliced
- Salt and pepper to taste
- Fresh cilantro for garnish
- Cooked rice or naan for serving

Instructions:

Marinate Chicken:
- In a bowl, combine the chicken pieces with curry powder, turmeric, cumin, coriander, salt, and pepper. Let it marinate for at least 15-20 minutes.

Sear Chicken:
- Heat vegetable oil in a large skillet or pot over medium-high heat. Add the marinated chicken pieces and sear until browned on all sides. Remove the chicken from the pan and set aside.

Sauté Aromatics:
- In the same skillet, add chopped onion, garlic, and ginger. Sauté until the onion is softened and aromatic.

Add Spices:
- Stir in curry powder, turmeric, cumin, and coriander. Cook for an additional 1-2 minutes until the spices release their fragrance.

Combine Chicken and Vegetables:

- Return the seared chicken to the skillet. Add diced potatoes and sliced carrots. Mix well to coat the chicken and vegetables with the aromatic spices.

Pour Coconut Milk and Broth:
- Pour in the coconut milk and chicken broth. Bring the mixture to a simmer. Reduce the heat to low, cover, and let it cook for about 20-25 minutes or until the chicken is cooked through, and the potatoes and carrots are tender.

Season:
- Taste and adjust the seasoning with salt and pepper as needed.

Garnish and Serve:
- Garnish the Coconut Milk Curry Chicken with fresh cilantro. Serve over cooked rice or with naan bread.

Enjoy:
- Enjoy this flavorful and creamy Coconut Milk Curry Chicken as a satisfying and aromatic meal.

Note:

- Adjust the level of spiciness by adding chili powder or red pepper flakes if desired.
- Customize the vegetables by adding bell peppers, peas, or spinach based on your preference.
- For extra richness, you can use full-fat coconut milk.

Tuna Casserole with Evaporated Milk

Ingredients:

- 8 ounces (about 2 cups) elbow macaroni or your preferred pasta
- 1/4 cup unsalted butter
- 1/4 cup all-purpose flour
- 1/2 teaspoon salt
- 1/4 teaspoon black pepper
- 2 cups evaporated milk
- 1 cup chicken or vegetable broth
- 2 cans (about 10 ounces each) tuna, drained
- 1 cup frozen peas
- 1 cup shredded cheddar cheese
- 1/2 cup breadcrumbs
- 2 tablespoons melted butter
- Fresh parsley for garnish (optional)

Instructions:

Preheat Oven:
- Preheat your oven to 375°F (190°C).

Cook Pasta:
- Cook the elbow macaroni or your chosen pasta according to the package instructions. Drain and set aside.

Make Roux:
- In a large saucepan, melt 1/4 cup of butter over medium heat. Add flour, salt, and pepper. Stir continuously to create a roux, cooking for 1-2 minutes until it becomes lightly golden.

Add Evaporated Milk and Broth:
- Gradually whisk in the evaporated milk and chicken or vegetable broth. Continue whisking until the mixture thickens and becomes smooth. Simmer for an additional 2-3 minutes.

Combine Tuna, Pasta, and Peas:
- Add drained tuna, cooked pasta, and frozen peas to the saucepan. Stir to combine, ensuring the ingredients are evenly coated in the creamy sauce.

Stir in Cheese:
- Stir in shredded cheddar cheese until it's fully melted into the mixture.

Transfer to Casserole Dish:

- Transfer the tuna and pasta mixture to a greased casserole dish, spreading it evenly.

Prepare Topping:
- In a small bowl, mix breadcrumbs with melted butter. Sprinkle this breadcrumb mixture over the top of the casserole.

Bake:
- Bake in the preheated oven for about 25-30 minutes or until the top is golden brown and the casserole is bubbly.

Garnish and Serve:
- Garnish with fresh parsley if desired. Let it cool slightly before serving.

Enjoy:
- Serve and enjoy this comforting Tuna Casserole with Evaporated Milk as a hearty and satisfying meal.

Note:

- You can customize this casserole by adding ingredients like diced mushrooms, celery, or onions.
- Feel free to experiment with different types of pasta based on your preference.
- Adjust the seasoning to your taste, adding herbs like thyme or dill for extra flavor.

Creamy Mushroom Risotto with Arborio Rice

Ingredients:

- 1 1/2 cups Arborio rice
- 1/2 cup dry white wine (optional)
- 4 cups chicken or vegetable broth, kept warm
- 2 tablespoons olive oil
- 1 small onion, finely chopped
- 2 cloves garlic, minced
- 8 ounces (about 2 cups) cremini or button mushrooms, sliced
- 1 cup wild mushrooms (e.g., shiitake or oyster), sliced (optional)
- 1/2 cup grated Parmesan cheese
- 1/4 cup unsalted butter
- 1/4 cup heavy cream
- Salt and black pepper to taste
- Fresh parsley, chopped, for garnish

Instructions:

Sauté Mushrooms:
- In a large pan or skillet, heat olive oil over medium heat. Add chopped onion and sauté until softened. Add minced garlic and cook for an additional 1-2 minutes until fragrant. Add sliced cremini or button mushrooms and wild mushrooms (if using). Sauté until the mushrooms are browned and cooked through.

Toast Rice:
- Add Arborio rice to the pan and toast it for about 2-3 minutes, stirring frequently to coat the rice in the oil.

Deglaze with Wine (Optional):
- If using wine, pour it into the pan and stir until the liquid is mostly absorbed by the rice.

Add Broth:
- Begin adding the warm broth to the rice one ladle at a time. Allow each ladle of broth to be absorbed before adding the next. Stir continuously to encourage the creaminess in the risotto.

Continue Cooking:
- Continue adding broth and stirring until the rice is creamy and cooked to al dente texture. This process usually takes about 18-20 minutes.

Finish with Butter and Cheese:
- Stir in unsalted butter and grated Parmesan cheese. Mix until the butter is melted, and the cheese is incorporated, creating a creamy texture.

Add Heavy Cream:
- Pour in the heavy cream, stirring to combine. This adds additional richness to the risotto.

Season:
- Season the creamy mushroom risotto with salt and black pepper to taste. Adjust the seasoning as needed.

Garnish:
- Garnish with fresh chopped parsley for a burst of color and freshness.

Serve:
- Serve the Creamy Mushroom Risotto immediately, offering additional Parmesan cheese at the table if desired.

Enjoy:
- Enjoy this luxurious and comforting Creamy Mushroom Risotto as a delightful main dish or a side.

Note:

- You can use various mushrooms according to availability and preference.
- If you prefer a non-alcoholic version, you can skip the white wine and continue with the broth.

Beef Stroganoff with Sour Cream

Ingredients:

- 1 pound (about 450g) beef sirloin or tenderloin, thinly sliced into strips
- Salt and black pepper to taste
- 2 tablespoons olive oil
- 1 onion, finely chopped
- 2 cloves garlic, minced
- 8 ounces (about 225g) cremini or button mushrooms, sliced
- 2 tablespoons all-purpose flour
- 1 cup beef broth
- 2 tablespoons Worcestershire sauce
- 1 tablespoon Dijon mustard
- 1/2 cup sour cream
- 1 tablespoon chopped fresh parsley, for garnish
- Egg noodles or rice, for serving

Instructions:

Season and Sear Beef:
- Season the thinly sliced beef strips with salt and black pepper. In a large skillet, heat olive oil over medium-high heat. Sear the beef strips until browned on all sides. Remove the beef from the skillet and set aside.

Sauté Onion and Garlic:
- In the same skillet, add chopped onion and cook until softened. Add minced garlic and sauté for an additional minute.

Cook Mushrooms:
- Add sliced mushrooms to the skillet and cook until they release their moisture and become golden brown.

Make Roux:
- Sprinkle flour over the mushroom mixture and stir to create a roux. Cook for 1-2 minutes to eliminate the raw flour taste.

Add Broth and Flavorings:
- Gradually pour in beef broth while stirring to create a smooth sauce. Add Worcestershire sauce and Dijon mustard. Bring the mixture to a simmer.

Return Beef to the Skillet:
- Return the seared beef strips to the skillet, coating them in the flavorful sauce. Let it simmer for 5-7 minutes until the beef is cooked through.

Finish with Sour Cream:
- Reduce the heat to low. Stir in sour cream, ensuring it is well combined with the beef and sauce. Cook for an additional 2-3 minutes until heated through.

Adjust Seasoning:
- Taste and adjust the seasoning, adding more salt and pepper if needed.

Garnish and Serve:
- Garnish the Beef Stroganoff with chopped fresh parsley. Serve over egg noodles or rice.

Enjoy:
- Enjoy this classic Beef Stroganoff with Sour Cream as a comforting and flavorful meal.

Note:

- For a richer sauce, you can add a touch of heavy cream along with or instead of sour cream.
- Customize the dish by incorporating your favorite herbs or a splash of white wine for added depth of flavor.

Sides:

Scalloped Potatoes with Gruyère Cheese and Milk

Ingredients:

- 2 pounds (about 900g) russet potatoes, peeled and thinly sliced
- 2 tablespoons unsalted butter
- 2 tablespoons all-purpose flour
- 2 cups whole milk
- 2 cups Gruyère cheese, shredded
- Salt and black pepper to taste
- 1/4 teaspoon ground nutmeg
- Fresh thyme leaves for garnish (optional)

Instructions:

Preheat Oven:
- Preheat your oven to 375°F (190°C).

Prepare Potatoes:
- Peel and thinly slice the russet potatoes. You can use a mandoline for uniform slices.

Make Béchamel Sauce:
- In a saucepan, melt the butter over medium heat. Stir in the flour to create a roux. Cook for 1-2 minutes until the roux is lightly golden. Gradually whisk in the whole milk, ensuring no lumps form. Cook the mixture until it thickens into a smooth béchamel sauce.

Add Gruyère Cheese:
- Stir in the shredded Gruyère cheese into the béchamel sauce. Continue stirring until the cheese is fully melted and the sauce is smooth.

Season:
- Season the sauce with salt, black pepper, and ground nutmeg. Adjust the seasoning according to your taste.

Layer Potatoes and Sauce:
- In a greased baking dish, layer the thinly sliced potatoes, slightly overlapping each other. Pour a portion of the Gruyère cheese sauce over the potato layer.

Repeat Layers:

- Continue layering potatoes and pouring sauce until all the potatoes and sauce are used. Ensure the top layer is covered with sauce.

Bake:
- Bake the scalloped potatoes in the preheated oven for about 45-50 minutes or until the potatoes are tender, and the top is golden brown.

Garnish:
- Optional: Garnish with fresh thyme leaves for a touch of herbaceous flavor.

Rest and Serve:
- Let the scalloped potatoes rest for a few minutes before serving. This allows the dish to set and makes it easier to slice.

Enjoy:
- Serve these Scalloped Potatoes with Gruyère Cheese and Milk as a rich and creamy side dish.

Note:

- Adjust the quantity of cheese according to your preference for a milder or more intense cheese flavor.
- Experiment with adding minced garlic or finely chopped onions to the béchamel sauce for additional depth of flavor.
- Ensure the potatoes are sliced uniformly for even cooking.

Creamed Corn with Whole Milk

Ingredients:

- 4 cups fresh or frozen corn kernels
- 1/4 cup unsalted butter
- 2 tablespoons all-purpose flour
- 2 cups whole milk
- 1 tablespoon sugar
- Salt and black pepper to taste
- Optional: Chopped fresh herbs (such as parsley or chives) for garnish

Instructions:

Cook Corn:
- If using fresh corn, remove the kernels from the cob. If using frozen corn, thaw it according to the package instructions. In a saucepan, cook the corn kernels until they are tender. If using fresh corn, this may take about 5-7 minutes; if using frozen, it will be quicker.

Make Roux:
- In a separate saucepan, melt the butter over medium heat. Add the flour and stir continuously to create a roux. Cook for 1-2 minutes until the roux is lightly golden.

Add Whole Milk:
- Gradually whisk in the whole milk, ensuring that no lumps form. Continue stirring until the mixture thickens and becomes a smooth sauce.

Combine Corn and Sauce:
- Add the cooked corn kernels to the milk sauce, stirring to coat them evenly.

Season:
- Stir in sugar, salt, and black pepper to taste. Adjust the seasoning according to your preference.

Simmer:
- Let the creamed corn simmer on low heat for an additional 5-7 minutes, allowing the flavors to meld and the mixture to thicken.

Garnish:
- Optional: Garnish the creamed corn with chopped fresh herbs, such as parsley or chives, for added freshness and color.

Serve:

- Serve the Creamed Corn with Whole Milk as a delicious and comforting side dish.

Enjoy:
- Enjoy the rich and creamy goodness of this classic Creamed Corn with Whole Milk.

Note:

- You can customize the sweetness level by adjusting the amount of sugar.
- For added depth of flavor, consider incorporating a pinch of ground nutmeg or a dash of cayenne pepper.
- Experiment with different herbs or spices to suit your taste preferences.

Mashed Sweet Potatoes with Brown Sugar and Milk

Ingredients:

- 3 large sweet potatoes, peeled and diced
- 1/4 cup unsalted butter
- 1/2 cup whole milk
- 1/4 cup brown sugar, packed
- 1/2 teaspoon ground cinnamon
- 1/4 teaspoon ground nutmeg
- Salt to taste
- Optional: Chopped pecans or marshmallows for topping

Instructions:

Cook Sweet Potatoes:
- Place the peeled and diced sweet potatoes in a large pot of water. Bring the water to a boil and cook the sweet potatoes until they are fork-tender, about 15-20 minutes.

Drain and Mash:
- Drain the cooked sweet potatoes and transfer them to a large mixing bowl. Mash the sweet potatoes using a potato masher or a fork until smooth.

Add Butter and Milk:
- Add the unsalted butter and whole milk to the mashed sweet potatoes. Continue mashing and mixing until the butter is melted, and the mixture is well combined.

Sweeten with Brown Sugar:
- Stir in the brown sugar, ground cinnamon, ground nutmeg, and a pinch of salt. Adjust the sweetness and seasoning according to your taste.

Blend Well:
- Mix the ingredients thoroughly, ensuring that the brown sugar is evenly incorporated into the mashed sweet potatoes.

Optional Toppings:
- If desired, top the mashed sweet potatoes with chopped pecans or marshmallows for extra flavor and texture.

Serve Warm:
- Serve the Mashed Sweet Potatoes with Brown Sugar and Milk warm as a delightful side dish.

Enjoy:
- Enjoy the sweet and creamy goodness of these mashed sweet potatoes as a comforting addition to your meal.

Note:

- Adjust the quantity of brown sugar and spices to suit your preferred level of sweetness and flavor.
- For a smoother consistency, use an electric mixer to blend the mashed sweet potatoes.
- Experiment with other toppings like a drizzle of maple syrup or a sprinkle of toasted coconut for added variety.

Cauliflower Gratin with Parmesan and Milk

Ingredients:

- 1 large head of cauliflower, cut into florets
- 2 tablespoons unsalted butter
- 2 tablespoons all-purpose flour
- 2 cups whole milk
- 1 cup grated Parmesan cheese
- 1/2 teaspoon Dijon mustard
- Salt and black pepper to taste
- 1/4 teaspoon nutmeg (optional, for additional flavor)
- 1 cup breadcrumbs (optional, for topping)
- Fresh parsley, chopped, for garnish

Instructions:

Preheat Oven:
- Preheat your oven to 375°F (190°C).

Cook Cauliflower:
- In a large pot of boiling salted water, cook the cauliflower florets until they are just tender. Drain and set aside.

Make Béchamel Sauce:
- In a saucepan, melt the butter over medium heat. Stir in the flour to create a roux. Cook for 1-2 minutes until the roux is lightly golden. Gradually whisk in the whole milk, ensuring no lumps form. Continue stirring until the mixture thickens into a smooth béchamel sauce.

Add Parmesan and Mustard:
- Stir in the grated Parmesan cheese and Dijon mustard into the béchamel sauce. Mix until the cheese is fully melted and the sauce is smooth.

Season:
- Season the sauce with salt, black pepper, and nutmeg (if using). Adjust the seasoning according to your taste.

Combine Cauliflower and Sauce:
- Gently fold the cooked cauliflower into the Parmesan béchamel sauce, ensuring the cauliflower is evenly coated.

Transfer to Baking Dish:

- Transfer the cauliflower and sauce mixture to a greased baking dish, spreading it evenly.

Optional Topping:
- Optional: Sprinkle breadcrumbs evenly over the top for a crispy topping.

Bake:
- Bake in the preheated oven for about 25-30 minutes or until the cauliflower is tender and the top is golden brown.

Garnish:
- Garnish the Cauliflower Gratin with chopped fresh parsley for a burst of color and freshness.

Serve:
- Serve the Cauliflower Gratin with Parmesan and Milk as a delicious and comforting side dish.

Enjoy:
- Enjoy the creamy texture and cheesy goodness of this Cauliflower Gratin as a tasty addition to your meal.

Note:

- Customize the dish by adding your favorite herbs or spices to the béchamel sauce for additional flavor.
- If you prefer a crispy topping, broil the gratin for a few minutes after baking to achieve a golden crust.
- Feel free to experiment with different types of cheese or a combination of cheeses for added variety.

Desserts:

Vanilla Panna Cotta with Berry Compote

Ingredients:

For Vanilla Panna Cotta:

- 2 cups heavy cream
- 1/2 cup whole milk
- 1/2 cup granulated sugar
- 1 vanilla bean or 1 teaspoon vanilla extract
- 2 1/4 teaspoons gelatin powder
- 3 tablespoons cold water

For Berry Compote:

- 2 cups mixed berries (strawberries, blueberries, raspberries)
- 1/4 cup granulated sugar
- 1 tablespoon lemon juice

Instructions:

For Vanilla Panna Cotta:

Prepare Gelatin:
- In a small bowl, sprinkle gelatin over cold water. Let it sit for 5-10 minutes to bloom.

Heat Cream and Milk:
- In a saucepan, combine heavy cream, whole milk, and sugar. If using a vanilla bean, split it lengthwise, scrape the seeds, and add both the seeds and the pod to the mixture. If using vanilla extract, add it later. Heat the mixture over medium heat until it is hot but not boiling. Remove the vanilla bean pod if used.

Dissolve Gelatin:

- Remove the cream mixture from heat. Add the bloomed gelatin to the mixture and stir until the gelatin is completely dissolved. If using vanilla extract, add it at this stage.

Strain Mixture:
- Strain the mixture to remove any undissolved gelatin or vanilla bean remnants.

Pour into Molds:
- Divide the mixture among your serving glasses or molds. Allow them to cool to room temperature, then refrigerate for at least 4 hours or until fully set.

For Berry Compote:

Prepare Berries:
- Rinse the berries and hull and slice any strawberries if needed.

Cook Berries:
- In a saucepan, combine the mixed berries, sugar, and lemon juice. Cook over medium heat, stirring occasionally, until the berries release their juices and the sugar is dissolved. Simmer for about 5-7 minutes until the mixture thickens slightly.

Cool Compote:
- Remove the berry compote from heat and let it cool to room temperature. Refrigerate until ready to serve.

Assemble:

Serve:
- Once the Vanilla Panna Cotta is fully set, spoon the berry compote over the top just before serving.

Garnish (Optional):
- Garnish with additional fresh berries or mint leaves if desired.

Enjoy:
- Serve and enjoy this elegant Vanilla Panna Cotta with Berry Compote as a delightful and indulgent dessert.

Note:

- You can use vanilla extract instead of a vanilla bean; add it after the gelatin is dissolved.
- Adjust the sugar in the berry compote according to your sweetness preference and the sweetness of the berries.
- Feel free to experiment with different berry combinations for the compote.

Tres Leches Cake

Ingredients:

For the Cake:

- 1 cup all-purpose flour
- 1 1/2 teaspoons baking powder
- 1/4 teaspoon salt
- 1/2 cup unsalted butter, softened
- 1 cup granulated sugar
- 5 large eggs
- 1 teaspoon vanilla extract
- 1/3 cup whole milk

For the Three Milks:

- 1 can (14 ounces) sweetened condensed milk
- 1 can (12 ounces) evaporated milk
- 1 cup whole milk

For Whipped Cream Topping:

- 1 1/2 cups heavy cream
- 1/2 cup powdered sugar
- 1 teaspoon vanilla extract

Instructions:

For the Cake:

Preheat Oven:
- Preheat your oven to 350°F (180°C). Grease and flour a 9x13-inch baking dish.

Sift Dry Ingredients:
- In a bowl, sift together the flour, baking powder, and salt. Set aside.

Cream Butter and Sugar:
- In a large mixing bowl, cream together the softened butter and sugar until light and fluffy.

Add Eggs and Vanilla:

- Add the eggs one at a time, beating well after each addition. Stir in the vanilla extract.

Incorporate Dry Ingredients:
- Gradually add the sifted dry ingredients to the wet ingredients, mixing until just combined.

Add Milk:
- Stir in the 1/3 cup of whole milk until the batter is smooth.

Bake:
- Pour the batter into the prepared baking dish and smooth the top. Bake for 25-30 minutes or until a toothpick inserted into the center comes out clean.

Cool:
- Allow the cake to cool completely in the pan.

For the Three Milks:

Combine Milks:
- In a bowl, whisk together the sweetened condensed milk, evaporated milk, and 1 cup of whole milk.

Poke Holes in Cake:
- Once the cake is cooled, use a fork or skewer to poke holes all over the cake.

Pour Milk Mixture:
- Slowly pour the three-milk mixture evenly over the cake, allowing it to soak in. Refrigerate the cake for at least 4 hours or overnight.

For Whipped Cream Topping:

Whip Cream:
- In a chilled bowl, whip the heavy cream until it begins to thicken. Add the powdered sugar and vanilla extract, and continue whipping until stiff peaks form.

Spread Over Cake:
- Spread the whipped cream over the chilled cake.

Serve:
- Slice and serve the Tres Leches Cake chilled. Enjoy the moist and creamy goodness!

Note:

- Customize the cake by adding a sprinkle of cinnamon or a drizzle of caramel sauce on top.
- Ensure the cake is completely cooled before pouring the milk mixture to allow it to absorb properly.
- The longer the cake sits in the refrigerator, the more moist it becomes.

Chocolate Pots de Crème

Ingredients:

- 6 ounces (about 170g) high-quality dark chocolate, finely chopped
- 2 cups heavy cream
- 1/2 cup whole milk
- 1/2 cup granulated sugar
- 6 large egg yolks
- 1 teaspoon vanilla extract
- Pinch of salt
- Whipped cream and chocolate shavings for garnish (optional)

Instructions:

Preheat Oven:
- Preheat your oven to 325°F (163°C). Place six ramekins or small jars in a baking dish, ensuring they are not touching.

Melt Chocolate:
- Place the finely chopped dark chocolate in a heatproof bowl. In a saucepan, heat the heavy cream, whole milk, and sugar over medium heat until it just begins to simmer. Pour the hot cream mixture over the chopped chocolate and let it sit for a minute. Stir until the chocolate is completely melted and the mixture is smooth.

Make Custard Base:
- In a separate bowl, whisk together the egg yolks, vanilla extract, and a pinch of salt until well combined.

Combine Mixtures:
- Slowly pour the chocolate mixture into the egg yolk mixture, whisking continuously to avoid curdling. Mix until well combined.

Strain Mixture:
- Strain the combined mixture through a fine-mesh sieve into a clean bowl to ensure a smooth texture.

Fill Ramekins:
- Divide the chocolate custard mixture evenly among the prepared ramekins or jars.

Bake in Water Bath:

- Place the baking dish with the filled ramekins in the preheated oven. Pour hot water into the baking dish, reaching about halfway up the sides of the ramekins, creating a water bath. This helps the custards cook evenly.

Bake until Set:
- Bake for about 30-35 minutes or until the edges are set, but the center is still slightly jiggly.

Chill:
- Remove the pots de crème from the water bath and let them cool to room temperature. Then, cover and refrigerate for at least 4 hours or overnight until fully chilled and set.

Garnish and Serve:
- Before serving, you can garnish with a dollop of whipped cream and chocolate shavings if desired.

Enjoy:
- Serve and enjoy these rich and silky Chocolate Pots de Crème as a decadent dessert.

Note:

- Choose a good-quality dark chocolate with a cocoa content you enjoy.
- If you prefer a smoother texture, you can blend the custard mixture before pouring it into the ramekins.
- Experiment with different toppings such as berries, mint leaves, or a sprinkle of cocoa powder for variety.

Rice Pudding with Cinnamon and Raisins

Ingredients:

- 1 cup long-grain white rice
- 4 cups whole milk
- 1/2 cup granulated sugar
- 1/4 teaspoon salt
- 1 teaspoon vanilla extract
- 1 teaspoon ground cinnamon
- 1/2 cup raisins
- Ground cinnamon for garnish

Instructions:

Rinse and Soak Rice:
- Rinse the rice under cold water until the water runs clear. In a bowl, soak the rice in water for about 30 minutes.

Cook Rice:
- In a medium-sized saucepan, combine the soaked and drained rice with 2 cups of whole milk. Bring to a simmer over medium heat, then reduce the heat to low, cover, and cook for about 15-20 minutes or until the rice is mostly cooked.

Add Sugar, Salt, and Vanilla:
- Stir in the granulated sugar, salt, and vanilla extract. Continue to cook over low heat, stirring frequently, until the rice is fully cooked and the mixture thickens.

Add Remaining Milk:
- Gradually add the remaining 2 cups of whole milk, stirring continuously. Cook for an additional 10-15 minutes, or until the rice pudding reaches your desired consistency.

Add Cinnamon and Raisins:
- Stir in the ground cinnamon and add the raisins. Continue to cook for another 5-7 minutes, allowing the raisins to plump and the flavors to meld. Adjust the sweetness and cinnamon according to your taste.

Cool and Chill:
- Remove the rice pudding from heat and let it cool for a few minutes. If you prefer it warm, you can serve it immediately. For a chilled version, refrigerate the rice pudding for at least 2 hours before serving.

Garnish and Serve:
- Sprinkle ground cinnamon on top before serving for an extra burst of flavor.

Enjoy:
- Serve the Rice Pudding with Cinnamon and Raisins either warm or chilled, enjoying the comforting and delicious flavors.

Note:

- You can adjust the sugar and cinnamon quantities based on your sweetness preference and taste.
- Feel free to customize the recipe by adding a pinch of nutmeg or cardamom for additional warmth and flavor.
- Experiment with different types of raisins or substitute them with chopped dried fruits for variety.

Coconut Rice Pudding with Mango

Ingredients:

- 1 cup jasmine rice
- 2 cups coconut milk
- 1 can (13.5 ounces) coconut cream
- 1/2 cup granulated sugar
- 1/4 teaspoon salt
- 1 teaspoon vanilla extract
- 1 cup diced ripe mango
- Toasted coconut flakes for garnish (optional)

Instructions:

Rinse and Soak Rice:
- Rinse the jasmine rice under cold water until the water runs clear. In a bowl, soak the rice in water for about 30 minutes.

Cook Rice:
- In a medium-sized saucepan, combine the soaked and drained rice with coconut milk, coconut cream, granulated sugar, and salt. Bring to a simmer over medium heat.

Simmer and Stir:
- Reduce the heat to low, cover the saucepan, and let the rice simmer for about 20-25 minutes or until it's cooked and the mixture has thickened. Stir occasionally to prevent sticking.

Add Vanilla:
- Stir in the vanilla extract and continue to cook for an additional 5 minutes. Adjust the sweetness according to your taste.

Cool and Chill:
- Remove the coconut rice pudding from heat and let it cool for a few minutes. If you prefer it warm, you can serve it immediately. For a chilled version, refrigerate the rice pudding for at least 2 hours before serving.

Dice Mango:
- While the rice pudding is cooling, dice the ripe mango into small, bite-sized pieces.

Serve with Mango:

- Serve the Coconut Rice Pudding in individual bowls, topped with diced mango.

Garnish (Optional):
- Optional: Garnish with toasted coconut flakes for added texture and flavor.

Enjoy:
- Enjoy this tropical Coconut Rice Pudding with Mango for a delightful and refreshing dessert.

Note:

- You can use arborio rice or other short-grain rice for a creamier texture.
- Adjust the sugar according to your sweetness preference.
- Experiment with other tropical fruits like pineapple or passion fruit for different variations.

Baked Goods:

Fluffy Buttermilk Biscuits

Ingredients:

- 2 cups all-purpose flour
- 1 tablespoon baking powder
- 1/2 teaspoon baking soda
- 1/2 teaspoon salt
- 1/2 cup unsalted butter, cold and cut into small pieces
- 1 cup buttermilk, cold

Instructions:

Preheat Oven:
- Preheat your oven to 450°F (230°C). Line a baking sheet with parchment paper.

Prepare Dry Ingredients:
- In a large mixing bowl, whisk together the all-purpose flour, baking powder, baking soda, and salt.

Cut in Butter:
- Add the cold, diced butter to the dry ingredients. Use a pastry cutter or your fingertips to quickly cut the butter into the flour until the mixture resembles coarse crumbs. It's okay if some larger pea-sized bits of butter remain.

Add Buttermilk:
- Make a well in the center of the flour mixture and pour in the cold buttermilk. Gently stir the ingredients together with a fork until just combined. Be careful not to overmix; the key to flaky biscuits is handling the dough as little as possible.

Knead and Fold:
- Turn the dough out onto a lightly floured surface. Gently knead it a few times, just until it comes together. Pat the dough into a rectangle and fold it in half. Repeat this process two more times.

Cut Biscuits:
- Pat the dough into a 1/2 to 3/4-inch thickness. Use a round biscuit cutter to cut out biscuits. Place the biscuits on the prepared baking sheet, making sure they are touching each other.

Bake:
- Bake in the preheated oven for 12-15 minutes or until the tops are golden brown.

Serve Warm:
- Allow the biscuits to cool for a few minutes on the baking sheet before transferring them to a wire rack. Serve the fluffy buttermilk biscuits warm.

Enjoy:
- Enjoy these delicious, flaky, and fluffy buttermilk biscuits as a side to your favorite meals!

Note:

- For even flakier biscuits, you can fold the dough a few more times during the patting and folding process.
- Handle the dough as little as possible to avoid tough biscuits.
- You can brush the tops of the biscuits with melted butter before baking for a golden finish.

Cream Cheese-Filled Banana Bread

Ingredients:

For Banana Bread:

- 3 ripe bananas, mashed
- 1/2 cup unsalted butter, melted
- 1/2 cup granulated sugar
- 1/2 cup brown sugar, packed
- 2 large eggs
- 1 teaspoon vanilla extract
- 1 1/2 cups all-purpose flour
- 1 teaspoon baking soda
- 1/2 teaspoon salt
- 1/2 teaspoon ground cinnamon

For Cream Cheese Filling:

- 8 ounces cream cheese, softened
- 1/4 cup granulated sugar
- 1 large egg
- 1 teaspoon vanilla extract

Instructions:

Preheat Oven:
- Preheat your oven to 350°F (175°C). Grease and flour a 9x5-inch loaf pan.

Prepare Cream Cheese Filling:
- In a mixing bowl, beat together the softened cream cheese, granulated sugar, egg, and vanilla extract until smooth and creamy. Set aside.

Make Banana Bread Batter:
- In a large bowl, mash the ripe bananas. Add melted butter and mix well. Stir in both granulated and brown sugars until combined. Add the eggs and vanilla extract, mixing until smooth.

Combine Dry Ingredients:
- In a separate bowl, whisk together the all-purpose flour, baking soda, salt, and ground cinnamon.

Incorporate Dry Ingredients:

- Gradually add the dry ingredients to the banana mixture, stirring until just combined. Be careful not to overmix.

Fill the Loaf Pan:
- Pour half of the banana bread batter into the prepared loaf pan.

Add Cream Cheese Filling:
- Spoon the cream cheese filling over the banana bread batter in the pan, spreading it evenly.

Top with Remaining Batter:
- Pour the remaining banana bread batter over the cream cheese filling, ensuring it's covered.

Swirl the Layers:
- Use a knife to gently swirl the cream cheese filling into the banana bread batter, creating a marbled effect.

Bake:
- Bake in the preheated oven for 60-70 minutes or until a toothpick inserted into the center comes out clean or with a few moist crumbs. If the top is browning too quickly, cover it with aluminum foil.

Cool:
- Allow the cream cheese-filled banana bread to cool in the pan for 10-15 minutes before transferring it to a wire rack to cool completely.

Slice and Enjoy:
- Once cooled, slice and enjoy this delicious Cream Cheese-Filled Banana Bread!

Note:

- Make sure the cream cheese is softened to avoid lumps in the filling.
- Customize the recipe by adding chopped nuts or chocolate chips to the banana bread batter if desired.
- Store leftovers in an airtight container in the refrigerator.

Lemon Poppy Seed Muffins with Greek Yogurt

Ingredients:

For the Muffins:

- 2 cups all-purpose flour
- 1 tablespoon poppy seeds
- 1 teaspoon baking powder
- 1/2 teaspoon baking soda
- 1/4 teaspoon salt
- 1/2 cup unsalted butter, softened
- 1 cup granulated sugar
- 2 large eggs
- 1 cup Greek yogurt
- 1 teaspoon vanilla extract
- Zest of 2 lemons
- 2 tablespoons fresh lemon juice

For the Glaze:

- 1 cup powdered sugar
- 2 tablespoons fresh lemon juice
- Zest of 1 lemon

Instructions:

Preheat Oven:
- Preheat your oven to 350°F (175°C). Line a muffin tin with paper liners.

Prepare Dry Ingredients:
- In a bowl, whisk together the all-purpose flour, poppy seeds, baking powder, baking soda, and salt. Set aside.

Cream Butter and Sugar:
- In a large mixing bowl, cream together the softened butter and granulated sugar until light and fluffy.

Add Eggs and Vanilla:
- Add the eggs one at a time, beating well after each addition. Stir in the vanilla extract.

Incorporate Greek Yogurt and Lemon:

- Add the Greek yogurt, lemon zest, and fresh lemon juice to the wet ingredients. Mix until well combined.

Combine Wet and Dry Ingredients:
- Gradually add the dry ingredients to the wet ingredients, mixing until just combined. Be careful not to overmix.

Fill Muffin Cups:
- Spoon the batter into the prepared muffin cups, filling each about two-thirds full.

Bake:
- Bake in the preheated oven for 18-20 minutes or until a toothpick inserted into the center of a muffin comes out clean.

Cool:
- Allow the muffins to cool in the tin for a few minutes before transferring them to a wire rack to cool completely.

Prepare Glaze:
- In a small bowl, whisk together the powdered sugar, fresh lemon juice, and lemon zest to create the glaze.

Drizzle Glaze:
- Once the muffins are completely cooled, drizzle the lemon glaze over the top of each muffin.

Enjoy:
- Enjoy these delightful Lemon Poppy Seed Muffins with Greek Yogurt as a tasty treat!

Note:

- Adjust the amount of lemon juice in the glaze to achieve your desired consistency.
- For an extra burst of flavor, you can add a little extra lemon zest to the muffin batter.
- Store the muffins in an airtight container at room temperature for freshness.

Chocolate Zucchini Cake with Sour Cream

Ingredients:

For the Cake:

- 2 cups shredded zucchini (about 2 medium zucchinis)
- 1/2 cup unsalted butter, softened
- 1/2 cup vegetable oil
- 1 3/4 cups granulated sugar
- 2 large eggs
- 1 teaspoon vanilla extract
- 2 1/2 cups all-purpose flour
- 1/4 cup cocoa powder
- 1 teaspoon baking powder
- 1 teaspoon baking soda
- 1/2 teaspoon salt
- 1 cup sour cream

For the Chocolate Ganache:

- 1 cup semi-sweet chocolate chips
- 1/2 cup heavy cream

Instructions:

Preheat Oven:
- Preheat your oven to 350°F (175°C). Grease and flour a 9x13-inch baking pan.

Shred Zucchini:
- Shred the zucchinis using a grater. Place the shredded zucchini in a clean kitchen towel and squeeze out any excess moisture.

Make Cake Batter:
- In a large mixing bowl, cream together the softened butter, vegetable oil, and granulated sugar until light and fluffy. Add the eggs one at a time, beating well after each addition. Stir in the vanilla extract.

Combine Dry Ingredients:

- In a separate bowl, whisk together the all-purpose flour, cocoa powder, baking powder, baking soda, and salt.

Incorporate Zucchini and Dry Ingredients:
- Gradually add the shredded zucchini to the wet ingredients, mixing well. Slowly add the dry ingredients to the zucchini mixture, alternating with the sour cream, beginning and ending with the dry ingredients. Mix until just combined.

Pour into Pan:
- Pour the batter into the prepared baking pan, spreading it evenly.

Bake:
- Bake in the preheated oven for 40-45 minutes or until a toothpick inserted into the center comes out clean.

Cool:
- Allow the cake to cool completely in the pan on a wire rack.

Prepare Chocolate Ganache:
- In a small saucepan, heat the heavy cream until it just begins to simmer. Pour the hot cream over the chocolate chips and let it sit for a minute. Stir until the chocolate is completely melted and smooth.

Pour Ganache:
- Pour the chocolate ganache over the cooled cake, spreading it evenly with a spatula.

Chill (Optional):
- If you prefer, refrigerate the cake for a short time to set the ganache.

Slice and Enjoy:
- Once the ganache is set, slice and enjoy this decadent Chocolate Zucchini Cake with Sour Cream!

Note:

- You can add chopped nuts or chocolate chips to the batter for added texture.
- Customize the ganache by adding a splash of vanilla extract or a tablespoon of butter for richness.
- Store any leftovers in an airtight container at room temperature or in the refrigerator for longer shelf life.

Custard-filled Pastries with Vanilla Glaze

Ingredients:

For the Custard Filling:

- 2 cups whole milk
- 1/2 cup granulated sugar
- 1/4 cup cornstarch
- 1/4 teaspoon salt
- 4 large egg yolks
- 2 tablespoons unsalted butter
- 1 teaspoon vanilla extract

For the Pastry Dough:

- 1 sheet puff pastry (thawed if frozen)

For the Vanilla Glaze:

- 1 cup powdered sugar
- 2 tablespoons milk
- 1/2 teaspoon vanilla extract

Instructions:

For the Custard Filling:

Prepare Custard:
- In a saucepan, heat the whole milk over medium heat until it just begins to simmer. In a separate bowl, whisk together the sugar, cornstarch, salt, and egg yolks until smooth.

Temper Eggs:
- Slowly pour a small amount of the hot milk into the egg mixture, whisking constantly to temper the eggs. Gradually add the tempered egg mixture back into the saucepan with the remaining hot milk.

Cook Custard:
- Cook the custard over medium heat, whisking continuously, until it thickens and comes to a gentle boil. Remove from heat, and stir in the butter and vanilla extract until smooth.

Chill Custard:
- Transfer the custard to a bowl, cover with plastic wrap (directly touching the surface of the custard to prevent a skin from forming), and refrigerate until fully chilled.

For the Pastry:

Preheat Oven:
- Preheat your oven according to the puff pastry package instructions.

Roll Out Pastry:
- Roll out the puff pastry sheet on a lightly floured surface. Cut it into squares or rectangles, depending on your preference.

Fill with Custard:
- Place a spoonful of chilled custard in the center of each pastry square. Fold the pastry over the custard, forming a triangle or rectangle, and seal the edges.

Bake:
- Place the filled pastries on a baking sheet lined with parchment paper. Bake according to the puff pastry package instructions or until the pastries are golden brown and puffed.

Cool:
- Allow the custard-filled pastries to cool on a wire rack.

For the Vanilla Glaze:

Prepare Glaze:
- In a bowl, whisk together the powdered sugar, milk, and vanilla extract until smooth.

Glaze Pastries:
- Once the pastries are fully cooled, drizzle the vanilla glaze over the top.

Serve:
- Allow the glaze to set, and then serve these delicious Custard-filled Pastries with Vanilla Glaze.

Note:

- You can dust the pastries with powdered sugar instead of using the glaze if you prefer a simpler finish.

- Experiment with different shapes and sizes for the pastries to add variety to your presentation.

Ice Cream and Frozen Treats:

Homemade Vanilla Bean Ice Cream

Ingredients:

- 2 cups heavy cream
- 1 cup whole milk
- 3/4 cup granulated sugar
- 1 vanilla bean (or 1 tablespoon pure vanilla extract)
- 6 large egg yolks

Instructions:

Prepare Ice Cream Maker:
- If using an ice cream maker, ensure the freezer bowl is frozen according to the manufacturer's instructions.

Split and Scrape Vanilla Bean:
- If using a vanilla bean, split it lengthwise with a sharp knife and scrape out the seeds. Place both the seeds and the scraped pod into a saucepan.

Heat Cream and Milk:
- In a saucepan, combine the heavy cream, whole milk, sugar, and the vanilla bean seeds and pod. Heat the mixture over medium heat until it reaches a scalding point (just before boiling), stirring occasionally. Remove from heat.

Infuse Vanilla:
- Allow the vanilla bean to steep in the hot cream mixture for about 15-20 minutes to infuse the flavor. If using vanilla extract instead, add it later.

Remove Vanilla Bean:
- Remove the vanilla bean pod from the mixture. If using vanilla extract, add it at this stage.

Prepare Egg Yolks:
- In a separate bowl, whisk the egg yolks until smooth.

Temper Eggs:
- Slowly pour a small amount of the hot cream mixture into the egg yolks, whisking constantly to temper the eggs. Gradually add the tempered egg mixture back into the saucepan with the remaining hot cream mixture, stirring continuously.

Cook Custard:
- Cook the custard over medium heat, stirring constantly, until it thickens enough to coat the back of a spoon. Do not let it boil.

Strain Mixture:
- Strain the custard through a fine-mesh sieve into a clean bowl to remove any cooked egg bits or the vanilla bean remnants.

Chill:
- Cover the bowl with plastic wrap, ensuring it touches the surface of the custard to prevent a skin from forming. Chill the custard in the refrigerator for at least 4 hours or overnight.

Churn Ice Cream:
- If using an ice cream maker, churn the custard according to the manufacturer's instructions until it reaches a soft-serve consistency.

Transfer to Container:
- Transfer the churned ice cream to an airtight container and freeze for a few hours or until it reaches a firmer texture.

Serve:
- Scoop and serve this delicious Homemade Vanilla Bean Ice Cream on its own or with your favorite toppings.

Note:

- If you don't have an ice cream maker, you can freeze the custard in a shallow dish, stirring every 30 minutes until it reaches the desired consistency.
- Experiment with adding mix-ins like chocolate chips, cookie pieces, or fruit to customize your vanilla ice cream.

Strawberry Swirl Frozen Yogurt

Ingredients:

For the Frozen Yogurt:

- 3 cups plain Greek yogurt
- 1 cup whole milk
- 3/4 cup granulated sugar
- 1 teaspoon vanilla extract

For the Strawberry Swirl:

- 2 cups fresh strawberries, hulled and sliced
- 1/4 cup granulated sugar
- 1 tablespoon lemon juice

Instructions:

For the Frozen Yogurt:

Prepare the Yogurt Mixture:
- In a bowl, whisk together the Greek yogurt, whole milk, granulated sugar, and vanilla extract until the sugar is fully dissolved.

Chill Mixture:
- Cover the bowl with plastic wrap and refrigerate the yogurt mixture for at least 2 hours or until thoroughly chilled.

For the Strawberry Swirl:

Prepare Strawberries:
- In a blender or food processor, puree the fresh strawberries until smooth.

Cook Strawberry Puree:
- In a saucepan, combine the strawberry puree, granulated sugar, and lemon juice. Cook over medium heat, stirring frequently, until the mixture thickens slightly. Remove from heat and let it cool to room temperature.

Create Swirl:
- Once both the yogurt mixture and strawberry swirl are chilled, alternate layering spoonfuls of the yogurt mixture and strawberry swirl in a container.

Swirl Layers:
- Use a spoon or a spatula to gently swirl the layers together, creating a marbled effect.

Freeze:
- Cover the container with a lid or plastic wrap and freeze the strawberry swirl frozen yogurt for at least 4 hours or until firm.

Serve:
- Scoop and serve the Strawberry Swirl Frozen Yogurt in bowls or cones.

Note:

- Experiment with different fruits for the swirl, such as blueberries, raspberries, or peaches, to create unique flavor variations.
- Add a handful of chopped nuts or chocolate chips during the last hour of freezing for added texture.
- Allow the frozen yogurt to soften slightly at room temperature for a few minutes before scooping for easier serving.

Mint Chocolate Chip Milkshakes

Ingredients:

- 2 cups vanilla ice cream
- 1 cup whole milk
- 1/2 teaspoon mint extract
- 1/2 teaspoon vanilla extract
- 1/2 cup chocolate chips
- Green food coloring (optional)
- Whipped cream and chocolate shavings for garnish (optional)

Instructions:

Prepare Blender:
- Place the vanilla ice cream, whole milk, mint extract, and vanilla extract in a blender.

Blend:
- Blend the ingredients until smooth and creamy.

Add Chocolate Chips:
- Add the chocolate chips to the blender and pulse a few times to mix them into the milkshake. You can leave some chocolate chips chunky for added texture.

Adjust Color (Optional):
- If you want a more vibrant green color, add a few drops of green food coloring and blend until well combined. Adjust the color according to your preference.

Pour into Glasses:
- Pour the mint chocolate chip milkshake into glasses.

Garnish (Optional):
- If desired, top the milkshakes with whipped cream and chocolate shavings for an extra indulgent touch.

Serve:
- Serve the Mint Chocolate Chip Milkshakes immediately with a straw or spoon.

Note:

- You can customize the mint flavor by adjusting the amount of mint extract to your liking.
- For a thicker milkshake, you can add more ice cream or reduce the amount of milk.
- Experiment with different types of chocolate chips, such as dark chocolate or mint-flavored chocolate, for a unique twist.

Cocktails:

White Russian Cocktail with Cream

Ingredients:

- 2 ounces vodka
- 1 ounce coffee liqueur (e.g., Kahlúa)
- 1 ounce heavy cream
- Ice cubes

Instructions:

Fill Glass with Ice:
- Fill an old-fashioned glass with ice cubes.

Add Vodka:
- Pour the vodka over the ice in the glass.

Add Coffee Liqueur:
- Pour the coffee liqueur over the ice and vodka in the glass.

Stir:
- Use a stirring stick or spoon to gently stir the ingredients in the glass, combining the vodka and coffee liqueur.

Top with Heavy Cream:
- Slowly pour the heavy cream over the back of a spoon or by drizzling it gently over the top of the drink. This will allow the cream to float on top of the cocktail.

Serve:
- Serve the White Russian cocktail with cream immediately. You can garnish with a sprinkle of cocoa powder or a coffee bean if desired.

Enjoy:
- Sip and enjoy this classic and indulgent White Russian cocktail.

Note:

- Adjust the ratio of vodka, coffee liqueur, and cream to suit your taste preferences.
- For a lighter version, you can use whole milk or half-and-half instead of heavy cream.

- Experiment with flavored vodka or different coffee liqueurs to create variations of the classic White Russian.

Irish Cream Liqueur

Ingredients:

- 1 cup Irish whiskey
- 1 can (14 ounces) sweetened condensed milk
- 1 cup heavy cream
- 2 tablespoons chocolate syrup
- 1 teaspoon instant coffee or espresso powder
- 1 teaspoon vanilla extract
- 1/2 teaspoon almond extract (optional)

Instructions:

Combine Ingredients:
- In a blender, combine the Irish whiskey, sweetened condensed milk, heavy cream, chocolate syrup, instant coffee or espresso powder, vanilla extract, and almond extract if using.

Blend:
- Blend the ingredients on high speed until the mixture is smooth and well combined.

Taste and Adjust:
- Taste the Irish cream liqueur and adjust the sweetness or flavorings if desired. You can add more chocolate syrup, coffee powder, or extracts to suit your taste.

Pour into Bottles:
- Pour the homemade Irish cream liqueur into sterilized bottles or airtight containers.

Chill:
- Seal the bottles and refrigerate the Irish cream liqueur for at least a few hours before serving. Chilling allows the flavors to meld and enhances the creaminess.

Shake Before Serving:
- Before serving, give the bottle a good shake to ensure the ingredients are well mixed.

Serve:
- Pour the homemade Irish Cream Liqueur into glasses over ice and enjoy.

Note:

- Adjust the level of sweetness by adding more or less sweetened condensed milk.
- Store the Irish cream liqueur in the refrigerator and consume within a few weeks.
- Feel free to experiment with the recipe by adding a hint of cinnamon, nutmeg, or other spices for additional flavor complexity.

Brandy Alexander with Nutmeg

Ingredients:

- 1 1/2 ounces brandy
- 1 ounce dark crème de cacao
- 1 ounce heavy cream
- Ice cubes
- Freshly grated nutmeg for garnish

Instructions:

Fill Shaker with Ice:
- Fill a cocktail shaker with ice cubes.

Add Brandy:
- Pour the brandy into the shaker over the ice.

Add Dark Crème de Cacao:
- Add the dark crème de cacao to the shaker.

Add Heavy Cream:
- Pour in the heavy cream.

Shake:
- Shake the ingredients well until the mixture is thoroughly chilled.

Strain into Glass:
- Strain the contents of the shaker into a chilled martini or cocktail glass.

Garnish with Nutmeg:
- Grate fresh nutmeg over the top of the Brandy Alexander for a delightful aroma and added flavor.

Serve:
- Serve the Brandy Alexander immediately.

Enjoy:
- Sip and enjoy the rich and creamy flavors of this classic cocktail.

Note:

- You can adjust the ratios of brandy, crème de cacao, and cream to suit your taste preferences.
- Experiment with different types of nutmeg for varying flavor profiles. Freshly grated nutmeg is recommended for the best aroma and taste.

Eggnog Martini with Spiced Rum

Ingredients:

- 2 ounces spiced rum
- 2 ounces eggnog
- 1/2 ounce simple syrup (optional, adjust to taste)
- Ice cubes
- Ground nutmeg for garnish

Instructions:

Chill Glass:
- Place a martini glass in the freezer to chill.

Fill Shaker with Ice:
- Fill a cocktail shaker with ice cubes.

Add Spiced Rum:
- Pour the spiced rum into the shaker over the ice.

Add Eggnog:
- Add the eggnog to the shaker.

Add Simple Syrup (Optional):
- If you prefer a sweeter cocktail, add simple syrup to the shaker. Start with a small amount and adjust to taste.

Shake:
- Shake the ingredients well until the mixture is thoroughly chilled.

Strain into Glass:
- Remove the martini glass from the freezer and strain the contents of the shaker into the chilled glass.

Garnish with Nutmeg:
- Sprinkle ground nutmeg over the top of the Eggnog Martini for a festive touch.

Serve:
- Serve the Eggnog Martini immediately.

Enjoy:
- Sip and enjoy the creamy and spiced flavors of this holiday-inspired martini.

Note:

- Adjust the amount of simple syrup based on your sweetness preference.
- For an extra touch, you can rim the martini glass with crushed graham crackers or cinnamon sugar before pouring in the cocktail.
- Freshly grated nutmeg can be used instead of ground nutmeg for a more intense flavor.